Nate & Shea's Adventures in SOUTH AFRICA

By Carrie Whitten-Simmons
with help and journal entries from
Nathan and Seamus, hosts of the television series
Travel With Kids

Look for QR codes like this throughout the book. Scan with your smartphone or tablet to see video of Nate & Shea's travels in Africa.
(May require QR code reader app.)

© 2014 Equator Creative Media In conjunction with *Travel With Kids* video series. All rights reserved. More information: www.TravelWithKids.tv

"Education is the most powerful weapon which you can use to change the world."
- Nelson Mandela

**Special thanks to
Terry, Holly, Michael, Wylder and Ella
and DSA Vacations.** Your enthusiasm and expertise on all things South Africa, with special attention to the detail required to planning a family trip, made our journey to South Africa amazing beyond our wildest dreams!

For more information, or to book your own journey to South Africa, visit:

www.DSAVacations.com

Molo! That means hello in Xhosa, one of 11 official languages of South Africa. With so many different people living there, the culture and history is fascinating. Plus, there are lions and cheetahs and rhinos, oh my! The nature here is unbelievable! Join us, Nate and Shea, hosts of television series *Travel With Kids*, as we discover a thing or two about South Africa and stop for lots of fun along the way!

Located at the southern tip of Africa, South Africa is flanked by two oceans - the Atlantic and the Indian. Its location along a major trade route has meant many different people coming together including Xhosa, Zulu, Setswana, Afrikaners, English, Dutch and more. From the earliest people in the world to some of the most recent government changeover, South Africa is loaded with history. In the wild, South Africa has cool animals like lions, rhinos and elephants and focuses on conservation.

Did you know...
- 3 of the 5 fastest land animals are found in South Africa
- South Africa has deepest mine in the world almost 3 miles deep
- World's first human heart transplant was done in South Africa
- The world's largest diamond was found in South Africa

In South African flag:
Black = African ethnicity
White = European ethnicity
Red = Wars/Soldiers
Blue = Skies
Green = Land
Yellow = Minerals (Gold)

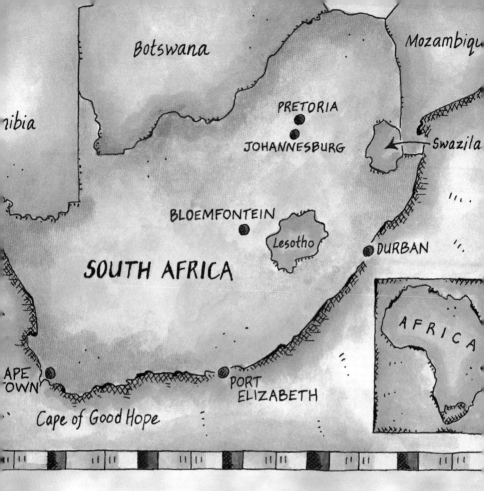

South Africa's west coast lies on the Atlantic Ocean; its east coast is on the Indian Ocean. It is about twice the size of France and surrounds the country of Lesotho. It has eight habitat types ranging from the Kalahari Desert in the north to grasslands to the Drakensberg Mountains in the east.

Safari

Cool Idea: Go on safari in your own backyard. Take pictures and make notes about all the creatures you find!

Many people go to South Africa to explore the grassland, savanna and bush on safari hoping to spot lots of animals. Not only did we see lots of animals, we saw them doing lots of cool stuff: rhinos fighting, leopards sneaking away from lions, jackals stealing a lion's dinner. Be sure to bring a camera and a journal to write down all the animals you see. There's also fun stuff to do like learn to track, make bows and arrows and cool places to stay like treehouses!

Treehouse Room Sabi Sands

Elephant dung baseball

Kruger National Park

South Africa has dozens of national parks and private game reserves, but the most famous is Kruger National Park. It is huge; almost the size of the U.S. state of New Jersey! The grasslands punctuated by streams, shrubs and thorn trees provide lots of shelter for the area's animals, which include the Big Five: Lion, leopard, Cape buffalo, African elephant and rhinoceros. It also has cheetahs, wild dogs, giraffes, hippopotamuses, zebras and more.

Coined by big game hunters, the Big Five is a list of the most dangerous animals to hunt on foot. Giraffes are not on the list.

Lion

Weighing about 400 ibs., the lion is the second biggest cat in the world! They live in groups called prides, which usually include females, cubs and a couple of males. Some males live like nomads, wandering and hunting on their own. Males have huge manes that make them appear bigger when they are fighting, but females do most of the hunting in the pride. Lions greet each other with a head rub and their roar can be heard from miles away.

Lion, Madikwe Game Reserve

Scan code to see the video

Rhinoceros

Like elephants, rhinos are large herbivores. There are two species of rhinos living in South Africa the white rhino and the black rhino. Both types are similar in color. The name may come from the size and shape of their lips; white sounds like the Afrikaans word for wide. Their horns can reach up to five feet in length. Rhinos have been hunted for that horn and are now endangered.

Rhinos Fighting Kruger National Park

Scan code to see the video

Leopard

Leopards are about half the size of lions. They live and hunt alone. They sleep in trees and are hard to spot. They are very strong, carrying large animals, like gazelles, into trees to eat. They are fast too, reaching speeds of 35 mph, but not as fast as cheetahs; a cat which looks very similar.

Leopard

Cheetah

The easiset way to tell the difference between leopards and cheetahs is by the black lines on the sides of the cheetah's nose.

Shea's Journal

Lions treed a leopard when we were on safari. I was glad that the leopard got away!

Leopard, Sabi Sands

Cheetah Conservation

walking with cheetahs
Tenikwa Wildlife Centre

Cheetahs are the fastest land animal in the world. They can reach speeds over 70 mph; that's about as fast as a car drives on the highway! Cheetahs are an endangered species with just over 10,000 left in the world. This is mostly due to conflict with people as we move into wilderness areas. It is rare to see cheetahs in the wild in South Africa, but there are several big cat conservation centers where you can meet rescued cats who cannot be returned to the wild due to injury or human contact. These centers help educate visitors as well as locals about ways to help save Africa's cats.

African elephant

African elephants are the largest living land animal. They can weigh as much as a small school bus! And, they are herbivores, which means they only eat plants. To keep all that weight on, they have to eat 500 lbs. a day. They use their trunks to pick food, give themselves a bath, suck up water to pour in their mouths, and to talk to each other. They live in very loving herds; when one gives birth the others touch the new mother with their trunks.

Elephant
Kruger National Park

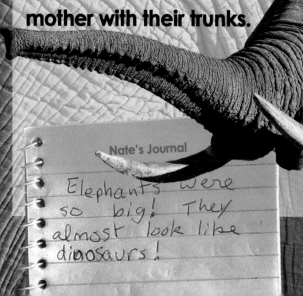

Nate's Journal

Elephants were so big! They almost look like dinosaurs!

Elephant Conservation

Throughout history elephants have been hunted for their ivory tusks. There is now a ban on ivory sales, but elephants are still poached, or hunted illegally. Elephant populations in Western Africa are still going down, but thanks to conservation efforts, Southern African herds are slowly growing. South Africa has several conservation parks where you can get to know elephants first hand. These are elephants that are used to human contact and cannot be returned to the wild.

Elephant Sanctuary, Plettenberg Bay

Cape buffalo

These guys are huge! They can weigh as much as a car and their horns can grow to three-feet across! They are very unpredictable, which makes them one of the more dangerous animals in Africa. They are also very loyal and will try to rescue a member of the herd who has been caught by a predator.

Buffalo Herd Kruger National Park

Ox-pecker birds keep a buffalo clean by eating parasites that live on its skin

Other African Animals

There are lots of loveable African animals beyond the Big Five. Relatives of the horse, zebras are known for their bad tempers and their stripes,  which are different on each animal. The stripes help them blend into tall grass and hide from predators. Giraffes are another popular animal to spot on safari. The tallest land animal, giraffes can grow up to 19 ft. tall! They use their long necks to reach food high up in the trees. They  also use them to fight. Their tongues are long too - sometimes almost two-feet long!

People of South Africa

Orginally South Africa was inhabited by San and Khoikhoi tribes. Later, the Nguni people - including Zulu, Xhosa, Swazi and Ndebele - from farther north arrived. Each tribe is recognizable through their various traditional dress, language and customs. Another large population includes European immigrants like English and Afrikaners - decendants of Dutch, French and German settlers. Later, laborers from China and India arrived.

Cradle of Humankind

Evidence of some of the world's oldest life - 3 billion year-old blue-green algae fossils and early dinosaurs - are found in South Africa. But, human fossils put it on the archeological map. In 1947, Dr. Robert Broom and John T. Robinson found a 2 million year-old fossil nicknamed *Mrs. Ples*. It is one of the earliest hominids ever discovered. In 1997, a full skeleton dating back over 3 million years was found. They are still uncovering fossils today. The Cradle of Humankind museum takes you on a journey through time and you can visit dig sites.

Mrs. Ples

Cradle of Humankind

Shea's Journal

It was cool to crawl through caves and see where archeologists were digging.

Scan code to see the video

Language

There are 11 official languages In South Africa. Many come from the original tribes that inhabited this land including isiXhosa, isiZulu, Setswana and Sesotho. Afrikaans and English are also widely spoken.

English	Afrikaans	Zulu	Xhosa
Hello	Hallo	Sawubona	Molo
Pronunciation:	Hah-low	Sow-bone-ah	Moh-low
How are you?	Hoe gaan dit?	Unjani?	Unjani?
Pronunciation:	Hoh-gon-deet	Oon-jah-nee	Oon-jah-nee
Good/well	Baie Goed	Ngikhona	Ndiphilile
Pronunciation:	Bye-hode	Nee-conah	In-dee-pee-lee-lay
Thank you	Dankie	Ngiyabonga	Enkosi
Pronunciation:	Donkey	Nee-ah-bone-ah	In-koh-see
Go Well (Bye)	Totsiens	Hamba kahle	Hamba kakuhle
Pronunciation:	Tote-seens	Hum-bah-gah-sleh	Hum-bah-kah-coo-hlay

The letters 'c', 'q' and 'x' are pronounced with clicking sounds in Xhosa and Zulu

Cultural Traditions

Since Zulu, Xhosa and other South African tribes originated from the Nguni people, many of their traditions are similar. For instance, both Zulu and Xhosa people believe that even after an ancestor dies, they are involved in the lives of their families. Many people visit a *sangoma*, or traditional healer, to talk with the spirit world for them. When a baby is born, it is introduced to the ancestors in a ceremony called *imbeleko*.

Xhosa ceremony to offer thanks to ancestors for rain in Kurland Village

Nate's Journal

I liked being part of the Zulu traditional dance. And their clothes are so colorful!

Zulu

Situated on the northeast coast, there are about 10 million Zulus in South Africa and it is the most widely spoken home language. The name Zulu means heaven. Under King Shaka, the Zulu became very powerful. During apartheid, Zulu people were moved to a region called KwaZulu. Traditionally, Zulus believe each human is made up of three parts: the physical, the energy and the personality and that the personality lives on after a good person dies.

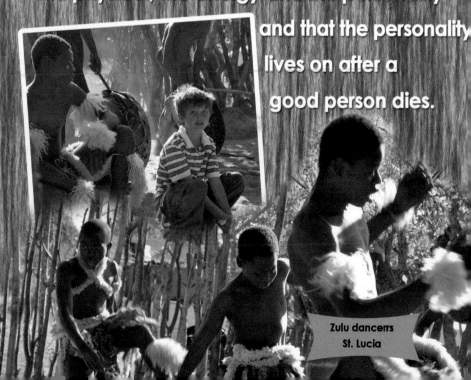

Zulu dancerrs
St. Lucia

Xhosa

Concentrated in the central south region, there are about 8 - 10 million Xhosa people, or "Red Blanket People", living in South Africa. isiXhosa is the second most popular home language. The *isiduko*, or clan, is very important to Xhosas. When Europeans first arrived, Xhosa people were hunter-gatherers who kept cattle. Their location between the settling Europeans and the Zulu tribes meant the Xhosa people saw a lot of fighting.

Famous Xhosas include:
Stephen Biko
Former Archbishop Desmond Tutu
Former President Nelson Mandela

Xhosa women
Plettenberg Bay

Bow & Arrow

Traditionally, hunting was done using a bow and arrow. Some rural communities still use them. It is fairly easy to make your own at home. Just get an adult's permission and be sure to only aim at a practice target and never at a person.

Bow:

Find a stick that is about four feet long and 1/2" in diameter. Scrape the bark off it and soak it in water for one day. Tie heavy twine to one end of the stick. Put the tied end on the ground, and push the top end down to create an arc shape. While it is in the arc, tie the twine to the top keeping the top pushed down and the twine as tight as possible. This may take two people one to hold the stick in arc shape and one to tie the twine.

Arrows

Find a few sticks that are about two feet long and 1/4" in diameter. Ask an adult for permission to use a knife and make a tip by sharpening the top of the stick. Starting about 2" from the tip, scrape the bark off in long motions towards the tip getting gradually narrower as you near the tip to create a point, like a pencil.

South African Food

One of the most traditional South African foods is called pap. It is a corn-based porridge. The kind we tried looked like mashed potatoes. Because of the laborers coming in during the 20th century, Indian and Chinese food is also popular. Bunny chow is a curry dish served in a loaf of bread. It was invented in Durban, South Africa. One of our favorite South African traditions is the braai. It is a type of barbeque with lots of different meats like steak, chicken, sausage and sometimes wild meat like kudu. Braai meats are often served with pap. Perhaps the most important ingredient of the braai is the spice used on the meat.

Braai Spice

1 TB salt
3/4 TB pepper
3/4 TB garlic powder
1/2 TB paprika
1 tsp chili powder
1 tsp cumin
3/4 tsp cloves
3/4 tsp nutmeg

Combine all ingredients using a pestle to crush if necessary. Use to season meats or as a dry rub before putting them on the braai, or barbeque.

Cape Colony

In 1652, the Dutch East India Company established a colony at the southwestern tip of Africa as a supply post and resting place for ships traveling the trade route from Asia to Europe. Under the control of Jan van Riebeeck, the colony grew as settlers moved inland for more land. In the 19th century, Britain ruled the Cape Colony. In 1910, the Union of South Africa formed as a British dominion with its Parliament in Cape Town. In 1961, the Republic of South Africa gained independence.

Scan code to see the video

Afrikaners

Afrikaners are Dutch, German and French settlers in the Cape Colony and Boers, settlers who left the colony. Boers are farmers who moved inland in search of more pasture land for their cattle and more independence from the Cape Colony. They had very different beliefs than the British people of the Cape Colony and they often fought. The Boers created their own republics, which were taken over by the Union of South Africa. Afrikaners speak Afrikaans, a language that comes from 17th century Dutch.

Cape Town

Started as the Cape Colony, Cape Town is now the second biggest city in South Africa and home of Parliament. It has famous landmarks like Table Mountain, which is the flat-topped mountain that soars above the city. You can hike up it or take a tram to the top. The Victoria & Alfred Waterfront in the port offers shopping, cafes and entertainment. We had fun riding the carosel and visiting Two Oceans Aquarium.

View from Table Mountain

Cape Peninsula

The Cape Peninsula extends south from Cape Town's Table Mountain. Its southern portion is the famous Cape of Good Hope. It is near here that the Atlantic and Indian Oceans meet. At its tip, you can stand on the most southwestern point in Africa. It is home to some very cute residents including penguins and baboons.

The Cape baboon, or chacma baboon, is one of the largest monkeys weighing up to 99 lbs. It's tall too...about 2 - 4 feet of body length and another 2 - 3 feet of tail. It lives in groups called troops which interact very similar to humans. You often see mother baboons carrying, scolding and grooming their babies.

Baboon, Cape Peninsula

Scan code to see the video

African Penguin

Boulders Beach, on the east coast of Cape Peninsula, is home to a colony of African Penguins. It is one of only three mainland colonies of this endangered species. There are 70,000 mated pairs of penguins, which is only about 10% of the population from 100 years ago. These penguins have a pattern of dots on their chest that is unique to each penguin, like a finger print to humans. They eat squid and fish and make a braying sound like a donkey.

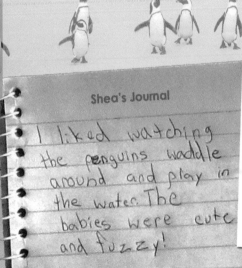

Shea's Journal

I liked watching the penguins waddle around and play in the water. The babies were cute and fuzzy!

Penguin, Boulders Beach

Great White Shark

One of the African Penguin's biggest predators is the great white shark. Most commonly found in the waters near Mexico, Australia, California and South Africa, this shark can grow over 20 feet long and weigh about 5000 lbs. That's more than most cars! Great whites eat seals, turtles and whales; humans are not on their menu.

Cage Diving, Gansbaii

Nate's Journal

It was amazing to see Great White Sharks so close. They were so graceful!

Scan code to see the video

Robben Island

Located a few miles north of Cape Town, Robben Island was the prison where political prisoners were kept during the struggle for racial equality. Several former presidents of South Africa spent time imprisoned here including Nelson Mandela who spent 18 years here. Mandela continued his fight for equal rights in prison as Africans were not given the same clothing and food as other people on Robben Island. Today, you can visit the prison on a tour given by a former inmate.

Scan code to see the video

Nelson Mandela's cell

Apartheid

Apartheid means "to live apart" in Afrikaans. It was a system of segregating people by race through laws passed by the National Party who ruled South Africa from 1948 - 1994. The government identified four classes of race: "black", "white", "coloured" and "Indian". From 1960 - 1983, more than three million non-whites were forced from their homes to live in race grouped areas. Education, health care and other public services were also segregated with lesser quality services being offered to non-whites. Apartheid ended in 1990 when the last apartheid law was repealed.

Relocation of Sophiatown, 1955

Nelson Mandela

Born into a Thembu royal family in 1918, Nelson Mandela was given the name Rolihlahla, which means troublemaker in Xhosa. Later, he was called by his clan name, Madiba, as a sign of respect. He had a very traditional Xhosa childhood and spent most of his days herding cattle. He attended school to become an advisor for the clan. He was involved in student government, boxing and cross country running. When he was 27 years old, he moved to Johannesburg where he worked as a law clerk and met fellow freedom fighter and friend Walter Sisulu.

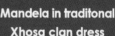

Mandela in traditonal Xhosa clan dress

In 1943, Nelson Mandela was part of a march to boycott bus prices. He then joined the African National Congress and began his most famous fight for equal rights for all people, regardless of their skin color. This fight landed him in prison, where he stayed for almost 30 years. When he was released by President F.W. de Klerk, Mandela secured free elections and preached forgiveness. In 1994, the first free elections, in which African people were allowed to vote, were held. Neslon Mandela was elected president. He formed the Truth and Reconciliation Committee, which he says "helped us move away from the past to concentrate on the present and the future". Mandela died at the age of 95 in 2013.

"I have cherished the ideal of a democratic and free society in which all persons will live together in harmony and with equal opportunities."
- Nelson Mandela

Other Freedom Fighters

Nelson Mandela was not alone in his fight for equal rights for all people. His political party, the African National Congress, included many people who were jailed or exiled for their protests including Walter Sisulu, Oliver Tambo, Bram Fischer and Thabo Mbeki, who was elected president after Mandela. Archbishop Desmond Tutu was also a huge voice in the fight against oppression. Known as "South Africa's moral conscience", he convinced the United States and Great Britain to stop trading with the apartheid government. After the end of apartheid, he called South Africa "the Rainbow Nation" because of all the races living together. In 1984, he won the Nobel Peace Prize.

> "Do your little bit of good where you are; it's those little bits of good put together that overwhelm the world."
> -Desmond Tutu

Desmond Tutu
Photograph by Benny Gool

Steve Biko

In the 1960s, Steve Biko's Black Conciousness Movement gained followers. Its slogan "Black is beautiful", tried to restore self confidence and a sense of self worth in African people. Biko said that African people had been put down for so long, they believed the negative things. He encouraged them to think positive about being African. In 1973, he was banned by the government, which meant his movements were restricted and he was not allowed to speak in public. Four years later, he died in police custody. Donald Woods, a white South African jounalist and friend, wrote a book about him called "Biko". It was made into a movie called "Cry Freedom".

> "Whites must be made to realize that they are only human, not superior. Same with blacks. They must be made to realize that they are also human, not inferior."
> -Steve Biko

Soweto Uprising

The fight against apartheid gained worldwide attention on June 16, 1976 when about 10,000 Soweto school kids marched to protest a new law that said subjects like math and social studies would be taught in Afrikaans. According to Desmond Tutu, this angered the students because it was "the language of the oppressor". When they reached a blockade, police officers fired shots and dogs were released. Thousands of people were wounded and almost two hundred were killed; the most famous was 13 year-old Hector Pieterson. This event had a huge impact in ending apartheid.

Nate's Journal

It is inspiring to know that kids helped change the world. WE RULE!

Scan code to see the video

> Home to the national football team, Soweto's FNB Stadium is the largest in Africa.

Soweto

Today, Soweto, or South Western Townships, is a peaceful place with many classes living side by side in homes ranging from low-income hostels to grand houses. Vilakazi Street is the only street in the world with the homes of two Nobel Peace Prize winners: Nelson Mandela and Desmond Tutu. You can visit Nelson Mandela's house and learn his story. Or, learn about the Soweto Uprising at the Hector Pieterson Museum.

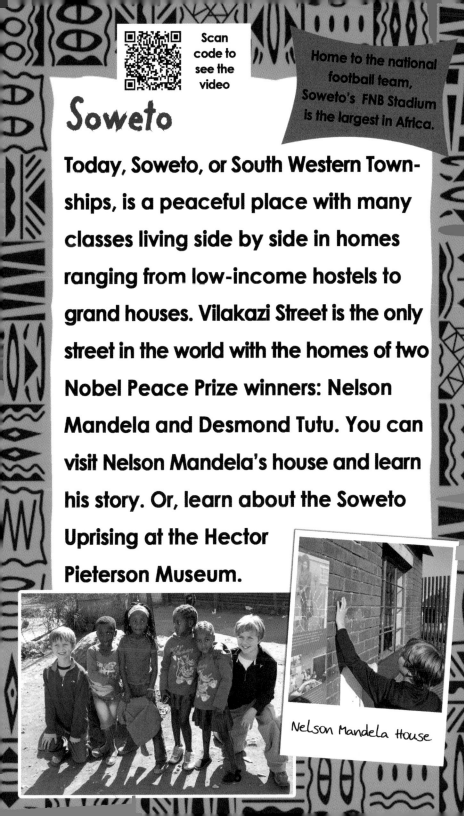

Nelson Mandela House

Sports

South Africans love sports. Football, or soccer as it is known in the U.S., is widely played. South Africa hosted the FIFA World Cup in 2010. Cricket is also very popular. But, the sport that South Africa is famous for is rugby. Their national team, the Springboks, won the 1995 World Cup. The team was embraced by Nelson Mandela after he became president. He used the team's competition in the World Cup, which was played in South Africa, as a unifying force for the country. This story was made into a book and later a movie called *Invictus*.

The springbok is a small antelope that can reach speeds over 50 mph and leap more than 10 feet

Now that you know a little bit about South Africa's people and animals, it's time to go check it out for yourself. We've made a list of our favorite animals - see if you can find them all. Whether you visit them from your computer at home or actually take a trip, enjoy your journey! To continue your South African vacation, check out the *Travel With Kids South Africa* video series.

Scan code for more info

Big Five

☐ Leopard

☐ Rhino

☐ Buffalo

☐ Lion

☐ Elephant

Ugly Five

☐ Marabou Stork

☐ Warthog

☐ Vulture

☐ Wildebeest
☐ Hyena

More Birds

☐ Flamingo

☐ Hornbill

☐ Ostrich

☐ Birdeater spider

☐ Stick Bug

Little Five

☐ Leopard Tortoise
☐ Rhino Beetle
☐ Buffalo Weaver Bird
☐ Antlion
☐ Elephant Shrew

Other Animals We Like

☐ cheetah

☐ zebra

☐ Giraffe

☐ Meerkat

☐ Serval

☐ Hippopotamus

☐ Vervet Monkey

Nate & Shea's Adventures provides information about destinations around the world. Learn history, culture and nature by taking a virtual trip with your guides Nate and Shea. *Nate & Shea's Adventures* can be used as a companion guide to the *Travel With Kids* video series or on their own.

Look for these other *Travel With Kids* products:

Nate & Shea's Adventures in:
Hawaii, South Africa, New York, Alaska Peru, London, Ireland, Wales, Italy, Florida

Travel With Kids (DVD):

United States:
Alaska
Florida
Hawaii: Oahu
Hawaii: Kaua'i
Hawaii: Maui & Moloka'i
Hawaii: Big Island
New York
San Diego

Caribbean:
Bahamas
Caribbean Cruise
Jamaica
Puerto Rico & Virgin Islands

Europe:
England
Greece
Ireland
Italy
London
Paris
Scotland
Wales

Latin America:
Costa Rica
Mexico: Yucatan
Mexico: Baja
Peru

Episodes covering additional destinations available on Hulu, iTunes, Amazon and more

Find out more at TravelWithKids.tv

Printed in Great Britain
by Amazon